Kuala Lumpur Travel Guide

Top 10 Things to See and Do

Anna Fichter

Table of Content

I. Introduction

Malaysia's capital, Kuala Lumpur, is an energetic city spilling over with significance and enthusiasm. Kuala Lumpur, conceivably the most impressive city in Southeast Asia, attracts travellers from wherever the globe with its exceptional culture, best-in-class workplaces, and a group of attractions.

Kuala Lumpur has something for everyone, from undeniable milestones and real attractions to best-in-class malls and clamouring night markets. Kuala Lumpur offers something for everyone, whether you're an expert glancing through the best street cooking, a gutsy looking throughout outdoors pursuits, or a social vulture speedy to dive into the city's past.

We'll take you on a visit through the best sights and less well-known diamonds of Kuala Lumpur in our overview of the Super 10 Things to See and Do. We're sure you'll find something in our summary that will get your innovative brain and outfit you with enduring memories, whether you're going strangely or returning for another experience.

The renowned Petronas Twin Zeniths, a masterpiece of contemporary plan that overpowers the skyline of Kuala Lumpur, are first on the summary. These eminent zeniths are a high need interest for anybody branching out to Kuala Lumpur because they give stunning city vistas from their discernment decks.

There are various unquestionable designs and verifiable focuses to visit for those looking for a more friendly experience. There are a couple of chances to learn about the city's rich history and legacy, from the Islamic Articulations Verifiable focus to the Public Display lobby of Malaysia.

Close to its social achievements, Kuala Lumpur is renowned for its culinary scene. The city is a foodie's satisfaction because of its changed people and a blend of social orders. Each taste is dealt with, from commendable Malay meals to Indian and Chinese food.

There are various decisions to find Kuala Lumpur's typical wonderfulness for individuals who like external games. There are a couple of climbing and nature ways of examining, recalling those for the Batu Caves and the KL Woods Eco Park.

A visit to one of Kuala Lumpur's many retail locales is a prerequisite for every journey there. There are many spots to buy trinkets and nearby careful work, from the mumbling Central Market to the luxurious shopping buildings of Bukit Bintang.

We believe that this guide gives you a general blueprint of the best attractions in Kuala Lumpur. We're sure you'll find something on our overview to make your journey to Kuala Lumpur outstanding, whether you're a first individual who goes through time or returning for another experience.

II. Petronas Twin Towers

The Petronas Twin Pinnacles, normally alluded to as the Petronas Pinnacles, are one of Kuala Lumpur's most well-known and conspicuous landmarks. These monstrous pinnacles are a portrayal of Malaysia's turn of events and innovation and are currently a well-known objective for guests.

The Petronas Twin designs are the most noteworthy twin designs on the planet, remaining at a surprising level of 451 meters in the focal point of Kuala Lumpur's central business region. Guests might appreciate staggering perspectives on the city and its environmental factors from the sky span that interfaces the pinnacles on the 41st and 42nd levels.

A directed visit through the Petronas Twin Pinnacles is accessible to visitors, and it incorporates stops at the sky span and the 86th-floor perception deck. The perception deck, which gives far-reaching perspectives on Kuala Lumpur, is a popular area for snapping pictures and absorbing the stunning view of the city.

A media show about the structures' development is remembered for the 45-minute visit through the Petronas Twin structures. The intuitive structures displayed at the Petronas Exhibition permit guests to become familiar with the structures' set of experiences and mechanical advancements.

Guests are prescribed to hold their tickets ahead of time to forestall dissatisfaction since passage to the Petronas Twin Pinnacles is tagged. Contingent upon the guest's age and whether they are a Malaysian resident or a worldwide traveller, the expense of the ticket differs. At the ticket counter at the foot of the pinnacles, tickets may likewise be purchased on the web.

Guests might exploit the many stores and diners housed inside the pinnacles notwithstanding the directed visit. At the foot of the pinnacles is the Suria KLCC retail shopping centre, which has an enormous determination of top-of-the-line merchandise and notable overall originators. Also, there are many feasting choices, from drive-through joints to upscale diners.

Around evening time, when the pinnacles are enlightened in a shocking presentation of lights, is one of the most outstanding times to visit the Petronas Twin Pinnacles. The pinnacles are a popular area to see the New Year's Eve firecrackers show in the city.

For everybody visiting Kuala Lumpur, the Petronas Twin Pinnacles are a priority sight.

The Petronas Twin Pinnacles are an image of Malaysia's desire and future vision, as well as a recognition for the country's prosperity, because of its bewildering level, stunning vistas, and rich history. A visit to the Petronas Twin Pinnacles is a must whether you're an admirer of design or designing or are simply looking for an exceptional and important experience.

III. Batu Caves

A great many travellers visit Batu Caverns every year, spreading the word about it as one of Kuala Lumpur's most well vacation destinations. The limestone slope known as Batu sinkholes, which has various caves and cavern sanctuaries, is only 13 kilometres north of the downtown area. The Sanctuary Cavern, which has various Hindu sanctuaries and must be arrived at by climbing a precarious flight of stairs of 272 stages, is Batu Caverns' essential draw.

The many caves and sanctuaries at Batu Caves might be investigated by walking by guests who need to encounter the region's amazing normal magnificence and study its social and strict significance. The Sanctuary Cavern specifically, which is supposed to be north of 400 million years of age, is a huge spot of commitment for Hindu admirers in Malaysia.

The tremendous sculpture of Master Murugan that welcomes guests at the Sanctuary Cavern's entry is the Batu Caverns' most extraordinary component. With a level of 42.7 meters, the sculpture is the tallest of its sort in the whole world. It is an astonishing sight to see and goes about as a reference point for neighbouring travellers.

The Dim Cavern and the Ramayana Cavern are just two of the caves and sanctuaries of Batu sinkholes that might be investigated notwithstanding the Sanctuary Cavern. The Dull Cavern furnishes guests with the chance to find out about the environment and geography of the locale and is home to various intriguing sorts of bugs and different animals. The Ramayana Cavern has clear lifelike models showing episodes from the Hindu awe-inspiring writing of a similar name and is committed to it.

While there is no charge to enter Batu Caverns, gifts to help with site upkeep are gladly received. At the caverns' entry, there are various merchants offering tidbits and keepsakes.

Guests genuinely should be educated that Batu Caverns might turn out to be very occupied, especially during the most active travel season. Moreover, because the caverns are adored by Hindu enthusiasts, it's urgent to dress properly while visiting. Wearing unobtrusive clothing and legitimate footwear is encouraged.

Anybody making a trip to Kuala Lumpur should visit the Batu Caverns. Batu Caverns is an extraordinary and captivating site that gives sightseers a window into the substance of Malaysia because of its stunning regular excellence, rich social heritage, and strict significance. Whether you seriously love history, climate, or religion, Batu Caverns is sure to affect every individual who visits.

IV. Merdeka Square

Kuala Lumpur's Merdeka Square, also known as Dataran Merdeka, is a significant historical site and is regarded as the centre of the city. It is situated in front of the Malaysian Ministry of Information, Communications, and Culture's administrative building, the Sultan Abdul Samad Building.

The square is renowned for its lovely green areas and distinctive flagpole, one of the largest in the world at a height of 95 metres. The flagpole was first built in 1957, the year Malaysia won independence from British colonial authority, and it continues to stand as a testament to the nation's freedom and pride.

Merdeka Square is home to several significant sites and monuments, including the flagpole, the Royal Selangor Club, the Kuala Lumpur City Gallery, and the ancient St. Mary's Anglican Cathedral.

A prominent members-only club with a long history that helped shape Kuala Lumpur, The Royal Selangor Club was established in 1884. The club's main structure is a superb illustration of British colonial architecture and has a breathtaking veranda looking out over the plaza.

Anyone interested in learning about the history and culture of the city must visit the Kuala Lumpur City Gallery. The gallery showcases a range of works of art and exhibitions that highlight Kuala Lumpur's rich cultural history, including its traditional crafts, architecture, and food.

A few minutes walk from Merdeka Square, St. Mary's Anglican Cathedral is one of Kuala Lumpur's most historic and beautiful cathedrals. The cathedral, which was constructed in the late 19th century and is renowned for its exquisite stained glass windows, has a spectacular Gothic Revival style.

Picnicking, jogging, and people-watching are just some of the outdoor activities that Merdeka Square visitors may participate in. The area is the ideal spot to unwind and take in Kuala Lumpur's ambience since it is surrounded by thick vegetation and gives breathtaking views of the city skyline.

Visitors can enter Merdeka Square whenever they want, and admission is free. For those who want to understand more about the background and importance of the many local sights and monuments, however, guided excursions are offered.

Anyone visiting Kuala Lumpur should make sure to stop at Merdeka Square. It provides guests with a unique and memorable view of the heart and spirit of the city with its rich history, gorgeous architecture, and lovely green areas. Merdeka Square is certain to make a lasting impact on everyone who visits, regardless of whether you are a fan of history, or culture, or just appreciate soaking in the beauty of your surroundings.

V. KL Bird Park

Adventurers who participate in the outside or are bird aficionados should visit KL Bird Park, generally called Taman Burung Kuala Lumpur. The unwinding locale, which is vehemently arranged in the midtown region and is home to two or three bird animal species from wherever on the planet, offers visitors a remarkable chance to associate personally with these captivating animals.

The entertainment space is organized in Kuala Lumpur's lovely Lake Nurseries region, a well-known voyager area and close central command. KL Bird Park, one of the most stunning bird parks on earth, is home to in excess of 3,000 birds from in excess of 200 species across a space of in excess of 20 segments.

One of the diversion locale's chief draws is the free-flight bird show, which is performed conventionally everyday and components different arranged birds doing astonishing achievements and stunts. Visitors could see the birds doing gymnastic achievements, rising above, and assisting their guides in a totally normal environment.

Another well-known development is the KL Bird Park's bird care gatherings, which license visitors to get extremely near a part of the interest's most stunning and excellent species. Visitors could purchase bird feed and subsequently hand-feed the birds for a magnificent and exceptional experience.

Despite the bird show and care get-togethers, KL Bird Park offers various activities and attractions, for instance, coordinated visits, a gift shop, and different bistros and bistros where visitors could loosen up and take in the staggering ecological components.

The Brahminy Land, one of the redirection district's most famous spots, is home to an arrangement of raptor creature gatherings, including owls, falcons, and flying hunters. Visitors could get a concise gander at these splendid birds as they take off above and show their incomprehensible abilities to hunt.

Another well-known locale is the Universe of Parrots, which is home to a shocking collection of amazing macaws and parrots. Seeing the associations between the birds and their tutors gives dazzling pieces of information about the social plans and individual direct norms of the birds.

KL Bird Park Entry is RM67 (about $16) for adults and RM45 (about $11) for youths. The expense of managing social occasions, watching the birds show, and other park parts are explored.

For individuals who could need to research the birds and their natural variables, coordinated visits are open for a cost. These undertakings are driven by educated and skilled visit pioneers who are learning about the different bird species and their approaches to acting.

At KL Bird Park, visitors are offered an attracting and totally open window to the spellbinding universe of birds, making it an outstanding and striking vacation spot. It is vital region for anybody visiting Kuala Lumpur on account of its staggering customary ecological components, important bird collection, and enchanting selection of activities and attractions. Whether you are a bird dear or just searching for a horseplay and informative family experience, KL Bird Park is guaranteed to enduringly affect each person who comes.

VI. National Mosque of Malaysia

Masjid Negara, in some cases alluded to as the Public Mosque of Malaysia, is a notable landmark in Kuala Lumpur. It is arranged in the focal point of the city and was developed in 1965 to respect the country's autonomy. Perhaps of the main construction in Malaysia, the mosque is a compositional marvel. The mosque draws sightseers from everywhere the globe and fills in as both a position of the petition and a critical vacationer location.

Area

In the focal point of Kuala Lumpur stands the Public Mosque of Malaysia. The mosque is arranged on Jalan Perdana, which is near the Perdana Professional flowerbeds and open by walking from various other popular traveller objections, including the Public Historical Center of Malaysia and the Islamic Expressions Gallery. Cabs, trains and different types of public vehicles may be generally used to get to the mosque easily.

Design

A wonder of design is Malaysia's Public Mosque. Three planners, Hisham Albakri, Baharuddin Kassim, and Arthur Benison Hubback, teamed up to make it. The mosque includes an unmistakable style that mixes contemporary engineering with traditional Islamic plans. A line of 48 segments supporting the mosque's umbrella-moulded shade act as a visual portrayal of Malaysia's 48 years of freedom. Up to 15,000 participants might fit in the mosque's fundamental supplication lobby, and there is a different petitioning heaven room just for ladies.

going to the mosque

Guests are wanted at the Public Mosque of Malaysia consistently from 9:00 am to 12:30 pm and from 2:30 pm to 4:00 pm. Before entering the mosque, guests should take off their shoes and dress unobtrusively. A headscarf is likewise required for ladies, and one is accessible at the mosque's entrance. There are directed voyages through the mosque that give vacationers a comprehension of its significance, history, and design.

Exercises at the Mosque

The Public Mosque of Malaysia fills in as an area for a few huge occasions as well as being a position of the petition. Muslim couples frequently decide to marry in the mosque, and the mosque's administration offers offices for the occasion. Moreover, the mosque is a popular area for the Eid al-Fitr and Eid al-Adha petitions, which draw a huge number of admirers. The mosque additionally has conversations and talks about Islam and its way of life for guests to join in.

Cost

It doesn't cost anything to enter Malaysia's Public Mosque. Guests are regardless asked to add to the mosque's upkeep and support thusly.

The Public Mosque of Malaysia is a huge milestone in Kuala Lumpur and a high-priority place for sightseers. As well as being a position of love, it is a masterpiece and an image of Malaysia's opportunity. For everybody inspired by Malaysian culture and history, it is a must-visit area because of its particular style and verifiable significance.

VII. Islamic Arts Museum Malaysia

Tourists interested in Islamic art and culture should definitely visit the Islamic Arts Museum Malaysia (IAMM). One of the biggest collections of Islamic art in the whole world is housed in this museum, which is situated in the heart of Kuala Lumpur. The IAMM's history, holdings, location, and entry costs will all be covered in this guide.

The Islamic Arts Museum Malaysia Foundation founded the institution in 1998, giving it a rich history. Its goal is to improve understanding and admiration of Islamic art and culture among the general population. The collection of the museum was built up via purchases, gifts, and loans made by individuals, collectors, and organisations all across the globe.

Collections: The museum's permanent collection has about 7,000 artefacts, including several works of Islamic art in the forms of textiles, pottery, calligraphy, metalwork, and more. The collection is broken up into twelve galleries and dates from the seventh century to the present. Each gallery showcases a certain component of Islamic art and is structured according to a theme. Among the most well-liked galleries are:

The Architecture Gallery: Models of outstanding Islamic structures from throughout the globe.
The Qur'an and Manuscripts Gallery features old and rare manuscripts, calligraphies, and Qur'ans.
Islamic textiles, including carpets, rugs, and costumes, are shown at the Textiles Gallery.

The Arms and Armour Gallery: Islamic historical armour and weaponry are on display.
Throughout the year, the museum also holds transient exhibitions that highlight various facets of Islamic art and culture.

Location: The Islamic Arts Museum Malaysia is situated next to the National Museum and the National Mosque in the heart of Kuala Lumpur. The KL Sentral Station is the closest station and offers easy access to the museum via public transportation. Visitors may then take a cab or the RapidKL bus to go to the museum from there.

Admission Fees: The Islamic Arts Museum Malaysia charges the following fees for entry:

Adults pay RM 14 Senior Citizens (60 years and over) pay RM 10 Students (with a valid

ID) pay RM 7 Children (below the age of six) pay RM 7 Free

For an additional cost, visitors can also purchase guided tours of the museum. The tours, which are led by museum professionals, provide guests a thorough look at the exhibits and galleries.

For travellers interested in Islamic art and culture, the Islamic Arts Museum Malaysia is a great choice. Visitors may learn about the wide history and variety of Islamic art by visiting the museum's subject galleries and large collection of artefacts. The museum is easily accessible to all tourists to Kuala Lumpur because to its convenient location and affordable entrance costs. Visitors to this museum will undoubtedly have a greater understanding of Islamic art and culture after their visit.

VIII. Central Market

One of Kuala Lumpur's most notable sights, Focal Market is arranged in the Chinatown area. The name Pasar Seni, which signifies "Craftsmanship Market" in Malay, is one more name for it. The market, which traces back to the 1880s when it worked as a significant junction for the trading of new natural products, is one of the city's most established landmarks. Today, Focal Market is a middle for culture and retail where guests can peruse for gifts while finding out about Malaysian customary expressions and specialities.

Area: Kuala Lumpur's Focal Market is situated at Jalan Tun Tan Cheng Lock. It is near other notable vacation spots including Petaling Road and the Sri Mahamariamman Sanctuary. An MRT station and many transport stations are nearby, simplifying it to utilize public travel to get to the market.

History: New meat, natural product, and fish were sold at Focal Market, which opened as a wet market in 1888. The market was remodelled in 1937 with Craftsmanship Deco components, and it ran as an ordinary market up until the 1980s. It was subsequently repaired and transformed into a business and social centre point. With its exuberant feel and conventional Malaysian expressions and specialities, the market is as yet a most loved objective for the two occupants and guests today.

Shopping: Malaysian-crafted works, including batik prints, wooden carvings, and customary garments, are generally accessible at Focal Market. Guests might examine the corners offering pottery, adornments, woven bushels, batik fine art, and other unmistakable tokens. The market likewise incorporates social exhibitions and craftsmanship displays, giving guests a knowledge of Malaysia's rich history.

cooking: The market likewise gives a scope of feasting options, including semi-formal cafés and customary Malaysian road food. Guests might look over cosmopolitan charges like Italian or Japanese food or neighbourhood claims to fame like nasi lemak, satay, and curry laksa. A phenomenal region to pause and refuel while seeing the city is Focal Market, which has a lot of sellers giving food and refreshments.

Diversion: Focal Market frequently coordinates far-reaching developments, for example, customary dance and music acts, allowing guests an opportunity to drench themselves in the nearby culture completely. To more deeply study conventional Malaysian expressions and specialities like batik painting and wood cutting, guests may likewise participate in courses and workshops.

Cost: Focal Market is a reasonable fascination, with most of the merchandise and dinners being presented at fair evaluation. Guests are asked to deal at the best costs since wrangling is boundless, especially while purchasing crafted works. There is no passage charge for the market or workshops or exhibitions from human expression.

Opening Times: Focal Market is available to individuals who wish to encounter the city whenever of the day since it is open consistently from 10 am to 10 pm. It is ideal to go on a work day since the ends of the week are frequently more occupied with the two occupants and guests.

For explorers who wish to find out about Kuala Lumpur's social history and purchase real Malaysian merchandise, Focal Market is a must-visit area. Guests might experience Malaysia's assorted social legacy in this bustling focus of action and vivid climate. Focal Market is a well-known objective for voyagers wishing to encounter the best of Kuala Lumpur given its open area, reasonable rates, and variety of food and shopping decisions.

IX. Chinatown

Anyone with any interest at all in deeply studying Kuala Lumpur's energetic culture and history ought to visit Chinatown, otherwise called Petaling Road, which is a clamouring area. Travellers from everywhere the globe view Chinatown as a captivating object due to its bustling commercial centres, beautiful structures, and delectable cooking.

Chinatown is arranged in the focal point of Kuala Lumpur, relatively close to the primary rail line station. For guests who like to stroll about the city, the area is a helpful objective since it is near open transportation.

History: The historical backdrop of Chinatown is extended and captivating. Chinese outsiders who showed up to Kuala Lumpur to work in the city's tin mines initially settled in the district in the nineteenth 100 years. With time, Chinatown formed into a flourishing business community, with shops offering everything from gadgets and trinkets to flavours and dresses.

Exercises: The Focal Market, a lively market where various things are sold, including handmade specialities, gems, and customary Malaysian food sources, is one of Chinatown's essential attractions. Guests may likewise peruse the numerous road slows down and restaurants in the area and test customary Malaysian dishes like nasi lemak, laksa, and satay.

The Sri Mahamariamman Sanctuary, a lovely Hindu sanctuary from the nineteenth hundred years, is another popular objective in Chinatown. The sanctuary offers visits where visitors might find out about its set of experiences and the significance of the area.

The KL City Exhibition is a priority area for history buffs. From Kuala Lumpur's earliest days as a mining town to its current situation as a bleeding edge, flourishing city, this gallery narratives the city's rich history.

A visit to the Petaling Road Night Market, a flourishing open-air market that comes to life in the evening, would adjust any visit to Chinatown. Guests might get all that they need here, including garments, road food, keepsakes, and amusement.

Value: most of Chinatown's attractions are either free or incredibly sensibly estimated. The Sri Mahamariamman Sanctuary is allowed to enter, and guests are allowed to peruse the commercial centres and road vendors during their relaxation. Anyone with any interest at all in more deeply studying the historical backdrop of the city ought to pay a little confirmation expense to the KL City Display.

By and large, Chinatown is a high-priority area for guests visiting Kuala Lumpur. Guests from everywhere the globe will without a doubt have a paramount involvement with this locale as a result of its captivating history, beautiful culture, and heavenly cooking.

X. Little India

In Kuala Lumpur, Malaysia, there is a clamouring and bright area called Little India. Sightseers who need to encounter the dynamic culture and customs of the Indian people group in Malaysia frequently go there. An interesting region to find, Little India is overflowing with sights, sounds, and fragrances that are ensured to stir your faculties in general. This guide will give you every one of the subtleties you need about Little India, including its set of experiences, focal points, area, and expenses.

The Little India story:

The start of Indian migration to Malaysia in the late nineteenth century is when Kuala Lumpur's Little India area started. As they made their homes all through the city, Little India at last turned into the focal point of the

Indian area. Today, it is a flourishing neighbourhood with countless foundations that serve Malaysia's Indian people group, including cafés, shops, and organizations.

Little India attractions include:

The most established Hindu sanctuary in Kuala Lumpur is called Sri Mahamariamman Sanctuary, and it is arranged in Little India. With its intricate carvings and clear tones, it is a wonderful sight to see. Entering the sanctuary to see the day-to-day supplications and functions is gladly received.

Masjid Jamek India is a shocking illustration of Indian Islamic engineering and is arranged in the focal point of Little India. The day-to-day petitions to heaven are available to the individuals who decide to enter the mosque.

Little India's primary lane, Jalan Tun Sambanthan, is a very busy place. Along its length are shops offering everything from gems and materials to snacks and customary Indian desserts.

The Focal Market is a phenomenal area to find Little India's rich culture. There are a few merchants there that give road food, keepsakes, and conventional Indian handiworks.

Sri Kandaswamy Kovil is a staggering Hindu sanctuary that should be visible in Little India. It is eminent for its choice of carvings and ravishing engineering.

Buddhist Sanctuary Brickfields Buddhist Maha Vihara is arranged in Little India. It is a peaceful shelter away from the jam-packed roads outside and a fabulous area to find Buddhist traditions and practices.

Whereabouts and Expenses:

Only a couple of kilometres south of the downtown area in Kuala Lumpur's Brickfields area is where you can track down Little India. Public travel, including the LRT and Monorail, simplifies it to arrive. Masjid Jamek India and the Sri Mahamariamman Sanctuary might be found on Jalan Tun Sambanthan, while the Sri Kandaswamy Kovil is arranged on Jalan Scott. On Jalan Travers, you can track down the Focal Market and Brickfields Buddhist Maha Vihara.

Contingent upon what you're looking for, Little India's costs could change. The expense of food and drinks is frequently generally sensible, with various road food merchants selling scrumptious Indian treats for a couple of ringgit. Costs for buys could fluctuate relying on the thing, but the Focal Market and Jalan Tun Sambanthan are incredible spots to get modest knickknacks and artwork.

Anybody visiting Kuala Lumpur who needs to drench themselves in the lively Indian culture and customs of Malaysia should come by Little India. There is something for everybody in this unique neighbourhood with its staggering sanctuaries, occupied roads, and scrumptious cooking. Little India is the best area to find out about Indian history, practice Indian religion, or simply partake in some heavenly Indian food.

XI. Sunway Lagoon Theme Park

Simply a short drive from Kuala Lumpur, in the Selangor suburb of Bandar Sunway, is the popular vacation location known as Sunway Tidal Pond Amusement Park. The recreation area is eminent for its elating rides, sea-going highlights, and an assortment of family-accommodating exercises. The recreation area, one of Southeast Asia's greatest amusement parks with an 88-section of land region, draws a large number of vacationers yearly.

Area
Only a short way from Kuala Lumpur is the Sunway Tidal Pond Amusement Park in Bandar Sunway, Selangor. It is open through the Government Interstate, the Lebuhraya Damansara-Puchong (LDP), and the KESAS (Kuala Lumpur - Shah Alam Motorway) expressways. To get to the recreation area,

guests might utilize a taxi, ride-flagging down administrations, or public travel like the KTM Komuter or BRT Sunway Line.

Cost

Contingent upon the bundle and the day of the week, different Sunway Tidal Pond Amusement Park tickets have various expenses. There are a few different ticket choices accessible at the recreation area, including yearly passes, family bundles, and public confirmation. Grown-up broad affirmation tickets are RM 139, while youngster tickets are RM 119. Family bundles for four individuals start at RM 496; yearly passes for grown-ups and kids start at RM 350 and RM 280, separately.

Attractions

A scope of attractions and exercises are accessible at Sunway Tidal Pond Amusement Park to suit the interests and periods of guests. A portion of the recreation area's popular attractions is recorded underneath:

The Vuvuzela, a quick water slide, and the FlowRider, a riding test system, are two of the water attractions at the water park. Families with little kids will likewise track down various pools, languid streams, and water jungle gyms properly.

Entertainment mecca - The Carnival offers various elating rides, for example, the privateer transport ride Hatchet and the topsy-turvy exciting ride Privateer's Vengeance. The merry-go-round and the Ferris wheel are two more quiet rides that are fitting for little kids.

Tigers, orangutans, and penguins are among the more than 150 sorts of animals that call the Natural Life Park home. Intelligent presentations and exhibitions let guests connect straightforwardly with a portion of the creatures.

Shout Park - Shout Park is a scary place and dismay zone fascination with a repulsiveness subject. It isn't prompted for little kids or individuals who are handily frightened.

Outrageous Park - The Outrageous Park has various heart-beating sports including bungee hopping, go-kart dashing, and paintball.

Shopping and Eating
There are a few eating decisions accessible at Sunway Tidal Pond Amusement Park, going from fast food to local cooking. All over the recreation area, guests might find food foundations including Burger Lord, Pizza Hovel, and KFC. There are various shops and gift stores that proposition attire, toys, and different merchandise.

Counsel to Guests

The accompanying counsel accommodated the individuals who need to visit Sunway Tidal Pond Amusement Park:

Dress serenely and put on outside action-fitting footwear.

For sun insurance, pack sunscreen, a cap, and shades.

To visit the water attractions, bring a difference in dress.

Before purchasing tickets, search for advancements and restricted time bargains on the recreation area's site.

To forestall swarms and extensive lines, arrive early.

One of Kuala Lumpur's top traveller objections is Sunway Tidal Pond, Amusement Park. Guests, everything being equal, may partake in the recreation area's numerous attractions and exercises, making their visit pleasant and noteworthy. Everybody might find something to appreciate at Sunway Tidal Pond Amusement Park, whether they like exciting exercises or family-accommodating shows.

XII. Conclusion

In conclusion, Kuala Lumpur offers visitors seeking culture, experiences, and entertainment a broad range of engaging activities. From the mind-boggling heights of the Petronas Twin Pinnacles to the serene surroundings of the KL Bird Park, there is something for everyone to enjoy.

Merdeka Square serves as a symbol of the nation's experiences and opportunities, while the Batu Caverns provide insight into Malaysia's social and supernatural history. The Islamic Expressions Exhibition Hall displays the elegance and superiority of Islamic craftsmanship, while Chinatown and the Central Market provide vibrant, bustling environments for dining and shopping.

Little India offers a unique opportunity for social interaction, while Sunway Tidal Pond

Amusement Park appeals to both families and thrill-seekers. The Public Mosque, a stunning and serene desert oasis in the city, should not be disregarded.

Kuala Lumpur is a must-visit location for anybody with even the slightest interest in learning about the rich history, culture, and general greatness of Malaysia. Given the abundance of things to see and do there, it is not surprising that this influential city is a sought-after destination for tourists. So prepare for a necessary trip in Kuala Lumpur by packing your bags and purchasing your tickets right now!